reMembering Mulatta

Christy Sampson-Kelly

Apprentice House
Loyola University Maryland
Baltimore, Maryland

Copyright © 2013 by Christy Sampson-Kelly

All rights reserved. No part of this book may be reproduced or transmitted in any form or by any means, electronic or mechanical, including photocopy, recording, or any information storage and retrieval system, without prior permission from the publisher (except by reviewers who may quote brief passages).

First Edition

Printed in the United States of America

ISBN: 978-1-934074-20-6
Ebook ISBN: 978-1-934074-23-7

Design by: Chloe Germain
Cover art by: Genevieve Sampson, fiberart

Published by Apprentice House

Apprentice House
Loyola University Maryland
4501 N. Charles Street
Baltimore, MD 21210
410.617.5265 • 410.617.2198 (fax)
www.ApprenticeHouse.com
info@ApprenticeHouse.com

Dedication

This is dedicated to my rebelliously reasonable parents for going against the script and obliterating, for me, this notion of choosing. Through their gracious allowance of my existence and growth within my in-between-ness, I continually become without diminishing any one of my-selves.

Contents

Dedication iii
Section 1: Once Bound 1
    Manuscript 3
    I Hope not to be Forgotten 4
    Knowing 6
    The Exchange of a Whisper 7
Section 2: Mis-placed 9
    Come Home 11
    A Cry in the Dark 12
    Deflecting Truth 13
    Vulnerability 14
    Lass 16
    Observation 18
    A Love not of this Earth 20
    Sleepless Night 22
Section 3: Re-dis-cover(y) 23
    Ensueño 25
    Other-than-Tragic Mulatta 27
    Sigh 28
    Re-birth 29
    Unfinished Visits by Accident 31

Section 4: Repentance 33
    Junior High Cafeteria 35
    Many 38
    Choice 39
    Wish 40
    Arrears 41
    Back Seat Meditation 42
    Deliverance 43
Section 5: A Reclaiming 45
    Waking in Winter 47
    The Poetics of Progeny 50
    Sacrificial Mounds 52
    This Day 53
    Ei's Fire 54
    Forgotten Bodies 55
    Vision of Cailleach 57
    Mosaic 58
    Death of the Great Writer 60
About The Author 63

Section 1: Once Bound

Manuscript

In ever changing conversation
collectively
we delve into present realities,
new awareness exposed.

In repetition,
boredom erased,
      more awe
      more wonder
      more dis-covered.

The weightless thread
that attaches my-self
to original understanding
still welcome.

Its litheness
compels past re-turns
fresh with possibility,
unwritten the time before.

I Hope not to be Forgotten

Where do I fit
in this mended world
stitched together by my people?

This world
of beautiful mahogany
so smooth and rich
one could get lost
in the feel of it.

This world
of dark knowing eyes
with knowledge so deep
that diving in
merely allows one
to tread at its surface.

This world
of thick, dense kinks
cropped short
revealing intricacy,
strength of character.

Where do I fit
with my buttery complexion
and devilish eyes,
with my overabundance
of sandy colored curls?

This I ask
in full support
of the reclaiming,
as mere reminder
that I exist.

Knowing

The twist of thinking's experience
begins belief's meander
for transcendent conceivers,
inescapably great thinkers.

While sauntering in gracious anticipation
of the welcoming,
understanding's verdant reach
acceptance's embrace.

Pondering how unmistakably heart-wrenching
it is to know.

The Exchange of a Whisper

somehow
it is different
although i can't be sure

my moves
definitely more intended
carefully constructed
to reveal only my true self

entering
it is unadulterated black
the moonless night
of a veiled village

troubled
i step in neither direction
for fear of losing

gently
a cool breeze
carrying your voice
tantalizes my spirit
reaching far inside
to existing places forgotten

drawing me deeper
i let it lead me

the essence of those
entering before
rushes through me
offering promises
escorting warnings

images of my own experience
so meticulously concealed
confront me
urging my retreat

reaching with-in
you are there
eyes, penetrating
skin, glistening sable

coming closer
We touch
and suddenly
all is lucid.

Section 2: Mis-placed

Come Home

Words echo
in a mind snowed under,
breathe
and I am home.

A screeching stop,
abounds short beings
into the street,
bitter cold wind abrading cheeks,
noses, foreheads.

Dashing toe spirits
unapologetically abandon their vessels,
leaving immobile, burdening stubs
at the ends of feet
presencing their absence.

A fleeting glance
through still, bitter air
expertly diverts my timid gaze from the ground
revealing our snow-covered roof.

A warm re-collection obliges me
to scale the mountain that is Albacon Road
through bodily memory alone
knowing another sighting
of my pending ascent
would re-present me here
on the out side of reverie.

A Cry in the Dark

Its piercing cry
swallows the serenity
of a room.

Requiring simply this
to destroy
what, in the aftermath
of their synchronization
seems so perfect.

One desperately grasping
to salvage
whatever
if anything
may be left.

The Other desperately grasping
to preserve
whatever
if anything
is to come.

Each helpless
in their implausible existence.

Suffering
as a result of something as trivial
as a cry in the dark.

Deflecting Truth

Illuminating whispers
possess the breathtaking power
of obscurity
with continual showing
of things unfamiliar
to words spoken.

Dark footpaths
wandered by bare feet
rely on uncommitted hands
to carry Diogenes' borrowed lantern.

Attempts to re-call humanness
are un-re-turned,
with facing nothing.

Not mother,
thoughtfully feeling her way
through this shadowy
and vexing terrain.

Not father
lost and stuck
in a multiflora rose bush
just east of the Bronx River.

Vulnerability

As he sits
letting the smooth melody he selected wash over him,
he is awed.

How could he
even for a moment
have believed
again.

Thinking back to the time before today,
when he last heard
that sweet voice.
The sound of it floods his mind
melting into the melody
emanating from his system.

Droplet
        by droplet
                he falls.

Starting first at his mouth,
then down his chest
and around his thighs
until finally
he is drenched
in thought.

He imagines penetrating eyes
the color of dawn
with golden flecks dancing through it.
Their fire warms him,
then gradually
becomes more and more heated,
causing an unleashing
of smothered desire.

Unable to satisfy it
he lay, letting it devour him.

Exhausted
he ventures one last thought,
upon whose entrance
a weak smile
adorns his face.

Contented with this
he drifts
into tranquility.

Lass

Voice travels
across the silent wailing air
of early morning,
well before sunrise.
Hoping desperately to convey meaning
to one already balancing
over a fragile state of affairs.

A soul thrashes furiously
beneath the encumbrance of weightless words
attempting to force a clenched mouth
to reveal all
its heart whispers.

How could one
have touched you so
causing the complete revelation and sharing
of your very self?

Spirit questions:
How could one
have risked all she knew
to start over
in places so foreign,
so unfamiliar?

Will shouts:
How could one
have taken in
your flesh to love and teach as her own
loving all that is you
and not you
undulating
beneath beaming innocence?

Choosing neither whisper
nor question,
nor shout
she lay,
knowing any of these
would only have complicated
this debut.

A slammed door
marks a dramatic exit
with thunderous applause
and at once
the universe turns in
and plainly states
that only a woman
could have selected mutism
for then.

Observation

Tiny bodies
suppressed for a time
that long since
should have come to close.

Individual desks
in symmetrical alignment
straightjackets
for curious hands,
belly laughs,
wiggly knees,
and happy feet.

Sitting,
watching...
my own thoughts
wander through the lace curtain
to the tree just outside the window.

Ash
one of the faery triad.
I search for oak and thorn.

The breeze tickles her leaves
meaning travels the air
boundedness, protection.

Struggle embodied
by shifting weight,
a bouncing knee,
all the while
still talking
ten minutes…
fifteen…

The one I have come for
catapults his from his seat
once,
twice,
three times
then…

freedom's secret sung
as footpath between
room and office,
my cheerless happy feet follow.

A Love not of this Earth

Inquiries met
with episodes
of harsh words,
spoken only by angry fists
thoughts,
thumped out with the rage of many
— alongside breath, sight, voice.

Turning to catch a lover's glare
through a stream of burning tears
unfamiliar, known eyes
reach out
their confusion meets only
with unnerving reflection.

Who am I?
asked of eyes full
with the tears of many
their hot, throbbing face smothered
with the sweetest of kisses.

This love
its nature further undraped
in new episodes
worse
in sporadic ceaselessness
is no longer willing.   I am gone.

Denial plays hard to get
prolonging misery's persistent chase
an un-relent-less hunt
over miles and miles
until desperate love dissipates
as it does
dispersing it's walking wounded.

One traipsing toward death
it's other trekking, toiling, transcending—still becoming.

Sleepless Night

The thickness of night
provokes me to a place
where my thoughts lie
in swirling silence.

I take the air,
moving about them
toward my intention.

A hurried foot slips
spilling the words and images
from one to another,
awakening us all.

It is now
that lying
next to the sound
of heavy, sleeping breath
makes me want to scream.

Section 3: Re-dis-cover(y)

Ensueño

telling me yours
now mine

sometimes a humid summer night
rustling autumn leaves
salt water
always a glass of coke with ice

and…

taken again
to possibility
re-placed

only slight dis-location
enough to
show my weakness
help you envision
through my woundedness
my vision then…
your implausible
beauty

precisely what
precision
couldn't master

reMembering Mulatta

me seeing
you seeing me
through suspiciously susceptible
blithely bountiful brown eyes
leaves me ajar
like city apartments
with unlatched deadbolts

needing,
mistaking
tenderness beneath your touch
for sorrow's revisit

instead of a hushed me
being quietly called back
to life

Other-than-Tragic Mulatta

Am I your greatest fear?

When you look at me,
do you perceive your-self
in combination
with your disquiet?

With my full, passionate lips
is my elfin nose
whispering in dead Gaelic tones.

With my bronzed skin
are my bulges and bends
leaping,
calling forth
in authentic primordial form.

Please do not turn away.
I welcome your looks.

It is in the brilliance of my splendor
that an indistinguishable flame ignites
within your essence
and beyond.

Sigh

In turning off the light,
darkness swallows her
and becoming it
she floats about
watching his moves.

He is picturesque.
The way his thighs crease in their strength
gently enveloping
her edge,
his smooth skin
pleasing the sheets so
that the pressure of his massive frame
not at all
disturbs them.

Shifting
in momentary discomfort,
he faces her.
In removing a wisp of her caressing hair
he cups her face
with a strong,
sure hand
and sighs a lifetime of relief.

Re-birth

The pride I feel as others admire
your round, full cheeks
and shapely thighs.

I grew those thighs.

First, as they lay inside of me
as I ate, you ate
as I breathed, you breathed.

Now, as you lay in my arms
taking in a cocktail created especially for you,
we look into one another's eyes
exchanging expressions and sounds.

We are one again,
if only for a while.
I think this a proper way to assist you
in becoming your-self
progressively allowing,
gradually accepting.

One of my favorite parts
is when something unexpected amuses you.
The corner of your mouth turns up,
leaking me down your cheek
as you smile.

Knowing that even after my body has lost its breath
and my spirit absconded,
I live on in your flesh.

Never
will you entirely be
without me.

Unfinished Visits by Accident

An invitation
over tea and cookies
peels back her-story
of college, mountain men,
uninvited development
and moving further in
to the mountain.

Giving the kids lunch,
the doorbell
announces a strange figure,
handshakes and introductions
become stories
of land, treestands, ethics,
NICU, cancer survival,
black and yellow labs.

Sitting out back with mom
in front of the rope swing,
an unfamiliar pickup
reveals requests to borrow our boy,
instead sending our man
he re-turns
with tales of hay bailing, ambition,
and lazy men sitting under their women.

Section 4: Repentance

Junior High Cafeteria

Bustling bodies,
noisy murmur of budding adolescent banter.

Swift movement through the babbling brook
places me in one of two streams of controlled movement.
Its current, hurried by obnoxious adult voices,
results in grabbing thoughtless rations.

Once a blissful drop of rain in my shameless singularity,
the confluence leaves me echoingly exposed
in this raging river of others.

I am wading,
treading,
beginning
to go under.

A familiar face at a sea of Those girls
strengthens my stroke in purpose,
dreaming calmer waters within reach.

I sit amongst them
adding to the whirlpool
swirling around the submerged, jagged rocks of he said, she said.

Suddenly
appearing at the mouth,
a good friend gone
for the last of the elementary summers.

My heart flutters
wanting to tell my stories
listen and listen to yours.

As our eyes meet,
the smile in my heart
fails its ascent to my face,
taken by the turbulence
of incorporation.

As you walk to an elsewhere
I cannot re-call now,
my last and strongest
memory of you in-forms itself…

The delta of that same river
days, weeks, a month later.
My surface worn smoother
an inside outsider
unsuspectingly naïve
- still -
to the policies.

My comment, disfigured
is released
and carried across borders.

"So, my legs are as black as my shoes?"

My unwanted response and balance depart,
taking with them
feeble attempts
to deflect the dragging undertow.

Those of Others join
in kicking when down
> black boots with a buckle
> sneakers with fat laces
> a pair of jellies

maliciously meet face, back, and belly
as hair is unmercifully stripped from its
two French braids.

Wondering occasionally
on islands
far from that day,
if you have any memory.

From the moment I did not,
wishing
I had smiled back.

Many

Many have had the misfortune
of encountering her.
Some drown unmercifully
in the depths of her eyes.
Some hopelessly bemused
in the maze of her edged words.

Still others,
clinging for dear life
slipped through fingers
and toes.

None found
she could sit
for hours
watching the delicate, purposeful moves
of a single bird,
that when she spoke thoughtfully
it was with the gentlest of lisps
or rocked herself nightly
into peaceful somber.

Unwilling to allow herself
to be dis-covered
by just any sojourner,
she eludes still
even the most veritable
of explorers.

Choice

Fearing punishment
for decisions made
a lifetime ago,
for harsh hands
sometimes dealt
to what was given,
for assuming
It
would be so easy.

Mostly for that lifetime,
as a result of which
you have given up on me.

Refusing to create
again
what I may choose to re-place.

I understand your dilemma.
Trust me now.
Things are not the same.
I am not the same.

Without answer
you only ache and bleed
all over again,
reminding me
of what I have put us through.

Wish

I long to be one of them
bending and swaying
in whatever direction
the winds choose to blow.

When the harsh summer rains
pound at their limbs,
they let it take them.
Only to emerge
lush and full
at the aftermath.

The luxury
of only imagining
the details
of my invader
escapes me.

I know every inch of him.

Arrears

I repay my debt to you
today
with a tearful of blood
from the innermost vessel
in the furthest reach
of what is me.

I know how it hurt
clawed at your intestines
and stung
as it flowed through every vein.
The slightest glint
kept you wanting
allowing you to deceive
even yourself.

At the careless whim of another,
I am reduced
to the shame that cuts
when I dare
to re-member you.

Back Seat Meditation

Choosing to sit next to my poetry,
I ride
and think of you.

She sings,
my spirit weeps
a bit.

This life seems designed
to leave no choices.

I blamed me
for loving so
and life
for its countless situations.

Now
a small part of me
tolerates secretly
behind strength and acceptance
imploring we each
can be happy enough
for us all.

Deliverance

She occupies us
again.

Her words
diminutive, flesh-dwelling glass shards
until extracted
by none Other,
than truth.

She winds
instability revealed,
unrest painfully apparent,
her contorted body
difficult to behold
without the luminescence of the moon
rendering her being
easier to bear.

He looks at her
full on
in broad daylight
and does not see her veracity,
but rather his cherub
draped in silk tulle,
round cheeks and wings,
time and potential.

She regards momentarily
perceiving stripped,
tormented remains
that make fixation impossible now.
It is only this
long awaited disentanglement
that keeps her mended.

Before all
it was her body
that cultivated,
and nurtured.
She can re-live afternoons
rocking
humming
pouring herself into
her cherub,
tending
those very cheeks and wings.

Instead,
it turns him inward to missed occasions
and shoddily patched wounds
grasping desperately
giving too much, too easily.

Disillusioned
by a reverie of hegemony,
he continually imparts
deliverance refused.

Section 5: A Reclaiming

Waking in Winter

Preferring the nighttime
alive, vigorously vibrant.
Suspecting, in another time
I am an owl,
quietly questioning by light
in solitude
exuberantly exploring by night,
the moon my guide.

This witching hour
keeps my sleepless body,
awake with thoughts of this day,
mostly of tomorrow,
sometimes of yesterday.

Leaping onto the bottom edge
of my twin-sized bed
she forces my legs to conform
to her form.

The warmth
of her heavy breathing
lulls me
to anticipated slumber.

Clack!

bright light
bitter breeze
cackling

Catching a glimpse
through sleep-filled eyes,
a slight profile
scurries from my doorway.

He is a finch,
the earlier the better
chirping, chattering, chiding, chasing,
he rises and falls with the sun.
Moaning loudly
pulling the blanket back over my head,
I could stay here forever.

Another presence.
Lights dim,
shades draw,
gentler light floods the room.

She folds the blanket down
revealing her face
gazing down at me,
our ritual begins
with my arm,
shoulder secured
before stretching, kneading
working her way to my hand,
manipulating small muscle
after muscle.

Feeling the warmth of blood
flowing outward
entering my fingertips,
the other arm
the other hand.

Stretching out my legs,
slowly opening my eyes,
feeling ready to brave
the icy floor that waits.

Time
to start a new day.

The Poetics of Progeny

i trust you today
with my fourth child
third born of my body
an-other work of art

uncomfortable
in clothes and shoes
i wish him to be
free and smiling
laughing even
the wind across his face

often preferring
grayed temples and wrinkles
wise, raspy voices
to the pudgy faces of his others
i wish his old soul quiet walks in open air
fanciful stories of seas, earth, and sky

so much of this world
is not that
instead, he is surrounded
by the machine-made objects of Abram
too loud—he covers his ears
too bright—he covers his eyes
he does not cope well
with the abrupt,
the unnatural

i am afraid of him collapsing into himself

do we go?
back to the farmhouse,
the cottage,
the cabin,
the asi
the world as his teacher

i have considered it
still…
considering it
secretly contemplating
whether bliss may only find him there

for now, though
i present him to you
naked,
head thrown back
in the middle
of a giggle
in hopes we are understood

—embraced even

supported in our journey
as he makes sense of this civilized world
as it is here, he must exist
at least for now

Sacrificial Mounds

Here I am
maimed they say,
betrayed by two
who so beautifully defined me.

Being without them
eyes still wander from my face
but not only those belonging to him
once reflecting
such empty wanting,
now it is both
his and hers
reflecting
fear,
wonder;
disgust,
amazement.

Seemingly unaware,
in childlike simplicity
—here I am.

This Day

Today I take the time
to re-collect,
to re-lease,
savoring all that we were.

It was our time.

We laughed!
How I adored your smile.
We loved
each other so…
We created
living testaments
to all that was good.

Looking at them
in their unblemished frailty
leaves no doubt
that we were meant to be.

You have given me,
I have given you,
we have given each other
the very best of our-selves.

In twilight,
we exist still
thriving, shining
in them.

Ei's Fire

Pondering its strength,
the words seem unworthy.

It is silence
unalterable, penetrating,
intangible, enveloping.

It is breath
essential, irrepressible,
inevitable, adamant.

It is fire
—elemental, uncontrollable, mesmerizing, consuming.

It is moonlight
illuminating, magical,
reflective of the radiance
that is you.

Forgotten Bodies

Disconnected,
searching for
wind
against face,
sun
warming skin,
earth
beneath bare feet,
a warm blanket
to be
under.

Always cold,

—as a child
part lizard
requiring the out-of-doors,
absorption of the sun's rays
—as an adult
iron deficient,
requiring words
scratched on personalized pads

Still,
striking at that certain angle
her beams transport me
to that more in-formed place,
of mucky terrain
rich with soil and tears

where the earth
swathes me
in her acceptance and care.

Vision of Cailleach

One day
she will appear
in white, untamed hair
swimming the river of my life,
telling its story while
rippling, undulating and circling.

Her dance
shoulders, hips, wrists
bare all of me
and more.

Mosaic

Used to blending in
wherever I go
I do not seem
to obtrude as something
distinct.

At the community dance
he asks why
my mother did not teach me how
to merengue.

Teen girls night out, listening
as a friend's friend complains incredulously
of being left
for a black girl.

In the office
just weeks after birth
he pleasurably regards us
promptly beginning our visit
in Tagalog.

At the fortieth birthday party,
the Ramapo Indian comment
mirthfully sails from her mouth
until I steal its wind.

In a way, I have been privy
to much that is private…
kept from those
who are perceived
to belong
to some well-defined collection.

Able to linger
on the periphery of the unfamiliar without offense,
much has been dis-closed to me.

Growing up longing
to have been cultivated
in a venerable pattern of knowledge,
beliefs, and
behavior,
I now honorably write
my story.

A diversity of place,
thought
taste
word
view
in-forming my being.

I am a mosaic of sorts.

Death of the Great Writer

How is it
that texts of great writers
take on lives
of their very own
making reading their notions
more like gazing through a diverging lens
as it brings about the extension
of rays of light into different directions
from their shared point of origination.

— the text itself engaging its visitor to un-cover, ex-tend, re-new

As we live out our day-to-day lives
in human be-ing,
in our surely perfect imperfection,
is then the dismissal of our poetics
somehow justified?

Is there a mis-take too grave
to promise redemption?

As we provide ourselves
up-to-the-minute ways to dissect lives,
can any face such intense scrutiny
and stand their enchanted ground?

In our continuous,
virtually instantaneous
access to her and his story
and resultant passing of judgment
are we depriving ourselves of inspiration?

If my words,
regardless of their beginnings,
audaciously, despite their intent
can move in benevolent greatness,
then are you not even more awed?

Look at what they have brought about.
Look at what you have seen in them,
have done with them.

What truer testimony
to our natural goodness
presents itself,
than poets toiling to live their words
in-the-world
making their attendance here
most human,
most engaging.

Perhaps choosing
to sway intimately in thought
over boisterous upheaval
is the choice of a differently constituted kind
and not the making of life's most celebrated.

Nonetheless, let us hold ever close
that with the breaking of each new day
our best is better.

If not, what then is life's purpose?

About The Author

Christy Sampson-Kelly is, amongst many things, a freelance writer and poet. The fragmenting and erasing of herself she experienced through instances of forced choice in the world outside her childhood home in New York, lead to countless hours of re-writing. It is no wonder her debut poetry collection, *reMembering Mulatta,* depicts a re-vision of everyday existence amid and beyond our sociopolitical construct of race.

Apprentice House is the country's only campus-based, student-staffed book publishing company. Directed by professors and industry professionals, it is a nonprofit activity of the Communication Department at Loyola University Maryland.

Using state-of-the-art technology and an experiential learning model of education, Apprentice House publishes books in untraditional ways. This dual responsibility as publishers and educators creates an unprecedented collaborative environment among faculty and students, while teaching tomorrow's editors, designers, and marketers.

Outside of class, progress on book projects is carried forth by the AH Book Publishing Club, a co-curricular campus organization supported by Loyola University Maryland's Office of Student Activities.

Eclectic and provocative, Apprentice House titles intend to entertain as well as spark dialogue on a variety of topics. Financial contributions to sustain the press's work are welcomed. Contributions are tax deductible to the fullest extent allowed by the IRS.

To learn more about Apprentice House books or to obtain submission guidelines, please visit www.apprenticehouse.com.

Apprentice House
Communication Department
Loyola University Maryland
4501 N. Charles Street
Baltimore, MD 21210
Ph: 410-617-5265 • Fax: 410-617-2198
info@apprenticehouse.com
www.apprenticehouse.com

www.ingramcontent.com/pod-product-compliance
Lightning Source LLC
Chambersburg PA
CBHW070451050426
42451CB00015B/3437